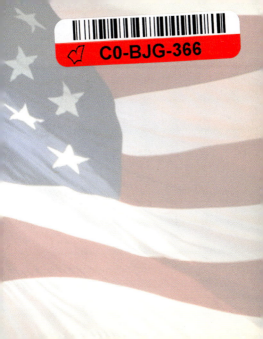

BROAD STRIPES & BRIGHT STARS

**Andrews McMeel
Publishing**

Kansas City

The flag is the en

sentiment, but of

the experience:

and women, tho

those who do and

odiment, not of istory. It represents made by men experiences of live under that flag.

WOODROW WILSON

A Brief History of the Flag

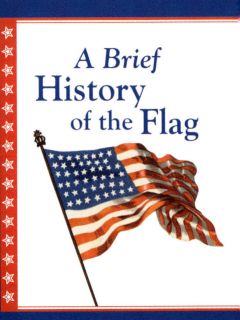

No one knows for sure who designed the first flag of the United States of America, or even who made it. Evidence in the records of the Continental Congress suggests that delegate Francis Hopkinson was the flag's primary designer.

Not many of today's historians believe that Betsy Ross was the first to sew one.

The first true American flag was the "Grand Union," which contained the familiar red-and-white bars, with the British Union Jack where the star field is presently. Once Independence had been declared the Union Jack was removed.

The earliest incarnation of our current flag had, in the star field, thirteen stars and the number "76" against a blue background. This was carried onto the field at the Battle of Bennington in August of 1776.

On June 14, 1777, the stars and stripes pattern was officially adopted by the Continental Congress, with the provision that each state would be represented by a single star.

In 1818, President James Monroe proclaimed that the stars representing new states would appear on the 4th of July after a state's induction into the Union.

But it was not until nearly a century later, in 1912, that the positions of the stars and general proportions of the whole flag were officially prescribed — by Executive Order of President William Howard Taft.

We Americans . . . bear
the ark of liberties
of the world.

MARK TWAIN

Liberty can not be preserved without general knowledge among people.

JOHN ADAMS

Liberty's too precious a thing

to be buried in books. Men

should hold it up in front of them

every single day of their lives and

say: I'm free to think and to speak.

My ancestors couldn't, I can,

and my children will.

Jimmy Stewart
Mr. Smith Goes to Washington

I don't measure America
by its achievement,
but by its potential.

SHIRLEY CHISHOLM

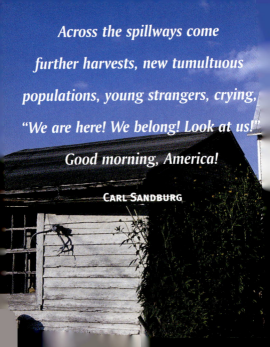

Across the spillways come

further harvests, new tumultuous

populations, young strangers, crying,

"We are here! We belong! Look at us!"

Good morning, America!

CARL SANDBURG

I love to look on

the stars and stripes. . . .

WALT WHITMAN

What makes the flag on
the mast wave? Courage!

Bert Lahr
The Wizard of Oz

America is a

willingness of the heart.

F. Scott Fitzgerald

The United States themselves ar

...essentially the greatest poem.

WALT WHITMAN

Whoever wants to know
the hearts and minds
of America had
better learn baseball.

JACQUES BARZUN

O beautiful for
patriot dream

That sees beyond the years

Thine alabaster
cities gleam

Undimmed by
human tears!

America! America!
God shed his grace on thee
And crown thy good
with brotherhood

From sea to shining sea.

KATHARINE LEE BATES
America the Beautiful

A thoughtful mind, when it sees a nation's flag, sees not the flag only, but the nation itself. . . .

HENRY WARD BEECHER

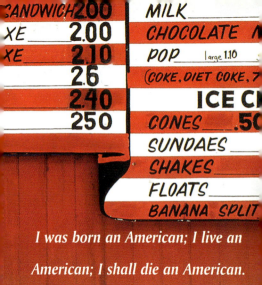

SANDWICH	200	MILK _____
XE ____	2.00	CHOCOLATE M
XE ____	2.10	POP _ large 1.10
____	26	(COKE, DIET COKE, 7
____	240	ICE CI
____	250	CONES ____ .50
		SUNDAES ____
		SHAKES ____
		FLOATS ____
		BANANA SPLIT

I was born an American; I live an American; I shall die an American.

DANIEL WEBSTER

Send these, the homeless,

tempest-tossed, to me

I lift my lamp beside

the golden door.

EMMA LAZURUS
Inscribed on the Statue of Liberty

Our flag is our national ensign, pure and simple, behold it! Listen to it! Every star has a tongue, every stripe is articulate.

ROBERT C. WINTHROP

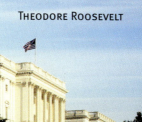

Americanism is a question of principle, of purpose, of idealism, or character; it is not a matter of birthplace or creed or line of descent.

THEODORE ROOSEVELT

Intellectually I know that America is no better than any other country; emotionally I know she is better than every country.

SINCLAIR LEWIS

America did not invent human rights. In a very real sense, human rights invented America.

JIMMY CARTER

Yes we'll rally around the flag,

boys, we'll rally once again.

Shouting the Battle Cry of Freedom.

GEORGE FREDERICK ROOT

I am still very much
of an American . . .
a believer in miracles.

HENRY MILLER

hat all citizens are brethren.

MARQUIS DE LAFAYETTE

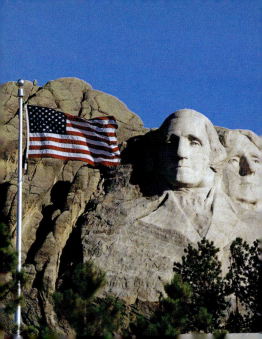

God and the politicians willing,

the United States can declare

peace upon the world, and win it.

ELY CULBERTSON

America was built on
courage, on imagination
and an unbeatable
determination to do
the job at hand.

HARRY TRUMAN

America is not merely
a nation but a
nation of nations.

LYNDON BAINES JOHNSON

There is a New America

every morning

when we wake up.

ADLAI E. STEVENSON

How to Fold the Flag Correctly

1. With another person, hold the flag parallel to the ground right side up. No part should ever touch the ground.

2. Fold the lower half of the stripe section lengthwise over the field of stars, holding the bottom and top edges securely.

3. Fold the flag again lengthwise, with the blue field on the outside.

4. Make a triangular fold by bringing the striped corner of the folded edge to meet the top edge of the flag.

5. Continue the triangular folding until the entire flag is folded in this manner.

6. When the flag is completely folded, only a triangular blue field of stars should be visible.

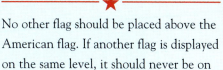

No other flag should be placed above the American flag. If another flag is displayed on the same level, it should never be on the right of the American flag.

The flag represents a living country, and is itself considered a living thing. It should not be lowered to any person or object. Nothing should ever be affixed to it or placed upon it, and it should not appear in advertising or as drapery.

No matter what the setting, the flag should always be displayed with the star field in the upper left corner. When displayed in a window, the side facing out should have the stars in the upper left.

The flag should never be used as covering for anything, even for a monument or a statue. A ceremonial flag is draped across the casket of veterans and public figures, and presented to the family at burial.

To fly the flag at half-staff, hoist it to the top and then lower it to half-staff. At the end of the day, raise it to the top before fully lowering it.

The flag is flown at half-staff upon the death of principal figures of the U.S. government. Following the death of other officials, the President issues specific procedure. For official instructions visit **www.whitehouse.gov**.

Broad Stripes & Bright Stars © 2002
by Smallwood & Stewart, Inc. New York City

For information, write Andrews McMeel Publishing,
an Andrews McMeel Universal company,
4520 Main Street, Kansas City, Missouri 64111.

ISBN: 0-7407-2515-7

Library of Congress Catalog Card Number:
2001098292

Designed by Curtis Potter

photo credits

★ **American Folk Art Museum:**
 page 18, *Flag Gate*. Artist unidentified.
 Jefferson County, New York, c. 1876. Paint on
 wood with iron and brass, 39.5″ x 57″ x 3.75″.